THE PASSIVE INCOME GUIDE
WHAT IS YOUR RETURN ON LIFE?

JOHN LARSON

Table of Contents

FOREWORD

Get real with me. How much does your employer pay you to quit your dream? Do you even remember what your dream was?

Most people get used to "settling" in life. When you were a teenager and thought about what your adult life would be like, I'll tell you one thing that you never thought: "I'm going to live a small life."

But now that's precisely what you've done.

So there you are, making between $70K and $150K, living life. You've got a good home and drive a decent car. Sometimes you feel "comfortable."

You don't vacation very often. You're sure to be in your cushioned swivel seat at your workstation at the appointed time each morning.

You sell your soul there at work. You tote company lines and occasionally play ridiculous charades to make it look like you're working, all just so that you can trade your time for dollars over-and-over again.

You've settled. You've even been programmed. You aren't even being yourself because you wouldn't naturally act that way.

In this one precious life that you've been given, you can't even be yourself!

Even if your job isn't so bad, is this really how you would choose to spend your time - if you could do anything in the world with your time?

Perhaps some of your dollars that you exchanged for your time are allocated into your 401(k) Retirement Savings Plan, or an IRA. They're often invested in mutual funds.

That's an awful thing to do with your money.

First of all, these vehicles are typically invested in stock and bond-based investments. Even if you feel like that's "going well," do you think that a 10% "paper," annual return is good?

Well, your plan administrator or financial advisor is not incentivized to tell you the whole truth.

From 10%, subtract out inflation, emotion, taxes, fees, and volatility, and you'll be lucky if your real return is as high as zero.

Did you know that 401(k)s were initially called "Salary Reduction Plans"? They had to scrap that name to foster employee participation. But reducing your salary today is principally what they still do to you.

Do you favor 401(k)s because you think that your money compounds on a tax-deferred basis, plus in retirement, you can pay a lower tax rate?

Well, that's the wrong strategy. In fact, you've just admitted failure.

Why?

Because you've just admitted that in retirement, you'll have a lower income, hence a lower tax rate.

Penalty-free withdrawals only begin between age 59.5 and 70.5. You must also start paying tax on them at that time. So you're certainly going to trade away pieces of your youth for a faint "hope" of having more in old age?

See, retirement plans are "Life-Deferral Plans" more so than "Tax-Deferral Plans."

"Retirement age" is when you'll finally have time to float the canals of Venice with your spouse, take the grandchildren to Disneyland, or buy and drive your Maserati. With more time to spend money, you'll want more income then, not less.

Plan for prosperity instead. Produce, don't reduce. Starting with a change in mindset, you can set up your life's finances so that your income increases both now and in perpetuity into the future.

Real estate has made more ordinary people wealthy than anything else. But few understand how.

You'll see that stocks usually only provide you with one way to profit. It's a capital gain if you buy and sell at the right time. Maybe you'll buy stock that pays a modest dividend too.

Real estate provides you with so many simultaneous profit centers: leveraged appreciation, cash flow, tenant-made principal paydown, greater tax advantages than stocks, and a way in which you actually profit from inflation.

When you understand this, you'll learn that total rates of return of under 20–25% are actually disappointing, and without taking inordinate risks.

In the stock world, that would be a blasphemous statement to make!

This is nothing new. This is just strategic buy-and-hold real estate investing.

Keep buying properties until you have enough cash flow (rent income minus property expenses) to replace your day job, and you can quit your job and declare financial freedom.

Remember 401(k)s...the "Salary Reduction Plan"? Now you've opted-in to a "Salary Increase Plan."

Now you've replaced your active income with passive income.

I have achieved this myself, so you can surely do it.

There are real estate pitfalls to avoid. That's why you're reading this book. Even when you buy right, some months, real estate investing can also leave you disappointed.

You need to begin with a sound strategy. You might be surprised to learn that in real estate investing, the property is only the fourth most important thing!

Instead, most people are misdirected and start their investment search with the property. They become emotional about landscaping, pretty window shutters, a bright red door, and quartz countertops. That's why they fail.

Soft emotions have a place in choosing your primary residence, but income property is about cold, hard facts.

First, the most important thing in investment real estate is YOU. Do you want real estate to provide you with appreciation, tax benefits, cash flow, or vacation use?

Secondly, once you're clear on "you," find the real estate market that will deliver what you want. "Market," could mean geography, neighborhood, or use type, for example, metro Kansas City, Philadelphia west of 49th Street, coastal Panama, single-family rentals, self-storage units, or four-plexes.

Thirdly, you must find a team that will deliver. Your most critical team member is a skilled, communicative property manager. You don't want to be the one collecting rents or taking tenant phone calls. You invest to enhance your quality of life, not degrade it.

Finally, only look at property fourthly. Because if those first three criteria don't work: you, market, and team - then your property criterion won't work either.

Don't get that part backward as most people do. Now you're being strategic.

I've come to know John Larson as the rare person that can deliver what you want. He understands markets, submarkets, teams, and properties. He knows that the property manager is the glue that holds your investment together over the long-term.

Shortly after I first met John in-person a few years ago, I was with him, and we were settled into his central office at American Real Estate Investments in Dallas, Texas.

Dallas-Fort Worth was - and still is - a thriving market. In fact, I think it's the most recession-resilient major metropolitan area in the United States.

But real estate prices had run up proportionally faster than monthly rent amounts, denting investor cash flow.

John and I were chatting alone together, and I asked him: "What will you do if the price disparity becomes so great that new investors could no longer produce monthly income?"

John replied: "I'd move into a new market."

That meant the world to me. Since then, John has shown me time and time again that he puts your investment interests ahead of the market.

Ethical operators like John can actually be disloyal to markets. They're loyal to people.

Real estate is the most historically proven investment class for wealth-building. Investors talk about ROI - Return on Investment.

With turnkey (done-for-you) real estate investing where you're in a vibrant market with sound management, you can also think of ROI as "Return on Involvement."

That's why you don't manage the property yourself. You don't want to track every little receipt yourself, lose weekends at Home Depot, or take tenant calls about replacing cove base or repairing a leaky faucet.

Invest in the right team. Now you'll have a high ROTI - Return on Time Invested. Whether life has taught you this yet or not, that's what you're really after.

John likes to call it a "Return on Life." I love that!

In this one life that you've been given, you can't afford to live below your means. You can instead use your faculties and efforts to expand your means.

Do you remember your daydream? Conjure it up and keep it alive. Now you have a vehicle to get there.

Die with memories, not dreams.

Real estate is the last frontier where you don't need a formal education to build passive income and achieve financial freedom incrementally. Get the freedom of time while you're young enough to enjoy it.

Though you might quit your day job, don't quit your daydream.

-Keith Weinhold of Get Rich Education

About Keith Weinhold

Keith Weinhold is driven by the mantra: "Don't Live Below Your Means. Expand Your Means". He owns GetRichEducation.com - groundbreaking original real estate investing podcasts, videos, and blogs to help you create financial freedom. Since 2014, his Get Rich Education podcast and app have created more passive income for people than nearly any show in the world. Keith's work appears in Forbes, Rich Dad Advisors, and Grant Cardone. He and his wife live in Anchorage, AK. He enjoys mountaineering and travel.

WHAT IS YOUR RETURN ON LIFE?

I think it's safe to say that most people feel they could use more free time—more "me time" for themselves. When you have a job, a busy family, kids with extracurricular activities, and so forth, time eats itself up quickly. Suddenly, you wake up one morning and think, "Whoa, I haven't golfed/hiked/watched a game/taken a nap in months!" And every aspect of your life blurs together. You're pulled in several directions, spread thin, and although you tell yourself you're doing well enough, could you be doing better? What if I told you that you could do better by doing less?

Wouldn't it be great if you could grow money? You can. I wish I could tell you how to plant a money tree! I can't. However, there's still some magic in what I am going to share with you.

When you put your money into a smart real estate investment or private lending opportunity, you reap cash flow, equity, and freedom. Yes, I'm talking about having more free time and having financial freedom as well. A passive real estate investment, specifically, is the most direct route to better living. Have you considered a vacation rental property? People line up to occupy it, and you can jet off to stay there any time you want. You can put your investment on autopilot and finally watch Sunday's game from the box (or the beach).

Passive real estate investments allow the investor to profit each month even though the property may be in another city, and somebody else (usually a team of pros) takes care of it. Although house-flipping shows and DIY projects sound exciting and fulfilling, they can increase the risk in a second. Even if you own just one single-family home, imagine how many things could go wrong with it, not to mention how much time you'll need to return it to the market.

What-ifs include a 2 a.m. phone call from a tenant, a pipe bursting overnight, a contractor doing a half-job before disappearing, or a tenant who is late on rent, again. Those problems eat more of your time, like Pac-Man gaining speed through the maze.

A commercial dwelling with twelve units looks like the money load, right? But twelve units equals at least twelve people to deal with, or you must find a property management company that can handle twelve units without smudging your bottom line. These options are anything but passive. They all require work, which takes even more of your time.

It's time to put your money to work so you can play. It's time to think outside the box, try something new—something with proven results and little effort. "What about the good ole stock market?" you ask. Sure, it works, but it's hardly passive. When it is passive, the returns are far less than those of real estate—where if you buy only one property, you will see a consistent, predictable return of 10 to 12 percent, annually. I could go on and on about selling options, tax benefits, and improved values over the long term, but I'll dive into those later. Right now, I want you to know that you can do this. Once you see the profits roll in, profits that can cover your owner-occupied mortgage, student loan payment, car payment, a couple of extra vacations, or triple your monthly savings deposit, life will look a lot more colorful.

HOW TO CREATE PASSIVE INCOME WITH REAL ESTATE

In the real estate market, you will discover several ways to make money, and these ways come with various levels of risk, reward, time, involvement, and satisfaction. Here are three bankable methods: single-family rentals and property management; private money lending, and lifestyle investing.

Single-family Rentals and Property Management

Turnkey real estate investing with the right company is a very hands-free way to earn passive income. In the right market, appreciation will create a steady increase in cash flow year-over-year and with a solid property management company behind it, your investment will provide you with peace of mind. If you are going to build a "passive" income rental portfolio, I advocate investing in homes valued at or close to the median value in that market. I have found that the farther you deviate below that median value, the more risk you take on, making the investment anything BUT passive. Homes in lower valued neighborhoods are more likely to run into thefts, vandalism, evictions, missed and late rental payments, and extended vacancies. When investing in true middle-class neighborhoods, your quality of tenant greatly increases, and crime is far less prevalent which results in a much more passive income-producing portfolio.

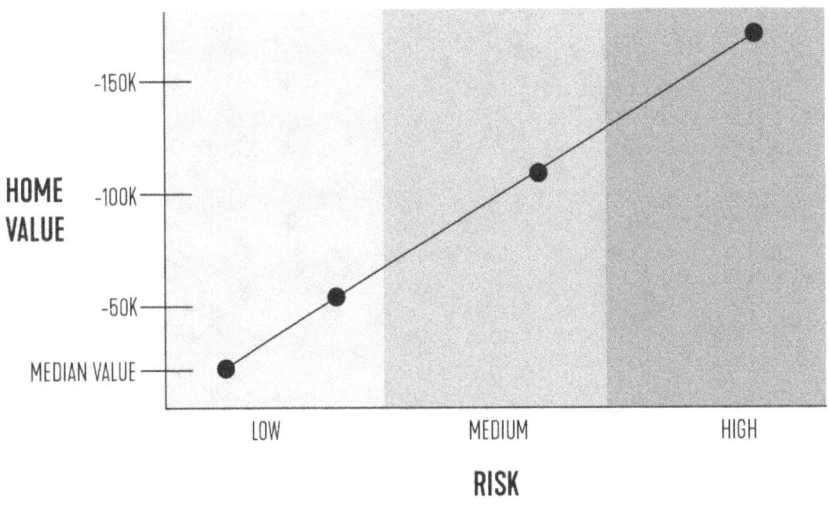

HOME VALUE vs. RISK

Private Money Lending

In the private money lending model, you become the bank, which is one of the safest and most passive investment models. Private money lending can offer you a very risk-averse, and in most cases, high rate of return with nothing to do except provide funding for residential or commercial development projects. Your return is paid out monthly at the annual rate, and at the end of the project, your initial investment is paid back with the option to reinvest in another project. Typically, when you are loaning on real estate development opportunities, you'll receive a deed of trust and a promissory note, making you an actual owner of the project. Private money lending is a very popular investment option for U.S. retirement account holders. Investors are increasingly discovering that they can self-direct their retirement funds and put them to work in investment opportunities that offer more control and higher fixed returns.

Lifestyle Investing

What if you were able to buy real estate in 1950s Hawaii? Imagine what kind of fun and financial legacy you would be leaving to generations of family. For real estate investors who want to use their property, investing in vacation property can give you the option to use when you want and earn when you don't. With full or fractional ownership opportunities, you can own a piece of paradise (beachfront condos, land lots for development, villas, and private islands). Each comes with full-service property management companies that secure occupancy and provide upkeep when you are not using the property. Invest in a lifestyle to create passive income through cash flow and appreciation.

WHAT IS TURNKEY REAL ESTATE INVESTING?

The term "turnkey" floats around quite a bit, especially when real estate agents are telling potentials buyers about a move-in ready property. The new owners can turn the key, and they're home free. It's that easy. When using this term regarding real estate investment, the same level of ease applies.

Typically, a property is purchased, renovated and upgraded, handed off to a property management company, and only then re-purchased by an investor. The property management company handles everything, including the placement of qualified tenants within the rental property and the day-to-day maintenance.

CREATING A TURNKEY PROPERTY

Before the investor signs a contract, the property needs to show potential cash flow and a high likelihood of appreciation (Year-Over-Year). The original buyer must look at the most progressive cities, neighborhoods, and markets perfectly primed for real estate growth. Here are a few things to consider:

- **Job Growth.** Employment is critical to the success of a community. Not only do investors want to see a low unemployment rate that either mirrors or is less than the national rate, but they want to see new job creation. The latter is a clear sign that companies are coming into the area and investing.

- **Population Size.** Small towns are quaint, but the demand for housing drops off quickly. Larger cities, especially those that offer new jobs, bring people into the area, which drives property values, sale prices, and rent. These cities also mitigate the risk of extended vacancy. Remember, these investments do not work unless you have someone consistently willing to pay you rent. Smaller towns or tertiary markets come with a greater vacancy risk.

- **Demographics.** Millennials and baby boomers are defining the population right now. The former is looking for career opportunities while the latter is searching for affordable, safe neighborhoods in which to retire. Markets with large groups of either population are ideal.

- **Infrastructure.** Is the area growing and receiving updates? Interstates, airports, parks, and old industrial sections are the telltale points of progress (or lack thereof). The market must have the ability to sustain the current population and future growth.

- **Median Sale Price.** One of the many measurements used for real estate market success is the sale price. Ideally, this price should be higher each time the property sells because

a) the market is thriving and b) the property is well maintained. Investors need to see the median sale price from year to year (comparing at least one to three years). The price should show increased value, but at the same time, be comfortably under the national average.

- **Exit Strategy.** Although your finances are in order today, the future is unknown. Buying riskier investments in stagnant or declining markets will not set you up for a strong exit strategy. Sophisticated investors serve themselves well with multiple exit strategies before investing in any opportunity. Therefore, I prefer to invest in properties that are priced close to the median value for the area and in markets that are increasing in population and job growth. This strategy allows for multiple exit strategies if the need to sell a property arises. Properties in true middle-class neighborhoods will also sell easily on the retail market to a retail homebuyer. Retail homebuyers do not care what the property rents for or what their return on investment is because they want to purchase a home in a desirable, sought after area.

An investor should investigate all factors, including the purchase price of the property and the average rental price in the area for such a property. The investor should experience an immediate cash flow within the first quarter. That is true turnkey investing.

THE DAY-TO-DAY MANAGEMENT

On paper, the investor doesn't have to lift a finger to maintain his or her property. Some circumstances require the "OK" from the owner, but for the most part, a property management company, or PM, takes care of everything. The investor can put his or her time and energy into other areas of interest, which is one of the most alluring qualities of this type of investment.

The PM handles advertising of the property, screening tenants, and getting the place occupied with little to no vacancy in between leases. The PM also maintains the property when it is vacant by cutting the grass, shoveling snow, and changing air filters. Repairs, replacements, and other urgent maintenance requests fall under the responsibilities of the PM. If the motor to the garage door breaks, the PM gathers repair estimates, sends them off to the owner and awaits his or her approval.

BUYER BEWARE

Because this scenario sounds so good, you need to beware. Several companies out there peddling "turnkey" investments lack the legs to make it stand up after closing. If you do your homework before purchase and pick up a property in a growing market, the rest is up to the

PM. Here are a few things to look for:

- **A Piece of the Pie.** The PM doesn't work for free, but the rate should be fair. The price should be somewhere between 8-10 percent of the monthly rental price (industry standard is usually 10 percent). The PM should be contracted to take care of everything, so the investor can easily live in another city or state.

- **Trust.** Ask for testimonials and look for reviews. Insist on a direct line of communication with the PM paired with quick responses. Ideally, a PM team consists of innovative financial professionals, former landlords, marketing experts, and experienced contractors.

- **Quality Upgrades.** Slap a little paint on and call it a renovation! Investors want to see high-quality upgrades, diligence, and a fully functioning house. From the foundation to the roof, all systems must be a-go with full disclosure on age and performance.

- **Maintenance Systems.** The potential investor can ask the PM for an explanation of operations. For example, how does the process go when a tenant places a maintenance request?

Check the back of the book for a list of questions to ask any potential property management partner before hiring them.

Legit PM companies and turnkey sellers are equipped to tackle the issues above and often supply the investor with even more information asked. An excellent PM is always forward-thinking, experienced and organized.

HOW TO LAND AN INVESTMENT PROPERTY

Establish a price point first. Narrow down the location to a region or two and begin to interview real estate investment companies. Investors can either purchase a property and assign it to a PM, or they can go through an agency that has a stock of ready-to-go investment properties and a PM team in place. The latter is a smoother approach—a company that can do everything for the investor, all in the same place.

Have the type of property in mind: a multi-family, a commercial building, a single-family house, etc. For those interested in a single-family home, for example, decide on a bedroom-bathroom ratio that supports young families or baby boomers who might have overnight family guests. In other words, the more bedrooms, the better! Other things to consider are the proximity to parks and interstates and the school district.

The purchase process of an investment property is very much like that of an owner-occupied home. The differences lie in the following.

- **Ownership.** Before signing the contract and grabbing the deed, investors may set up an LLC. The property can go under the LLC versus the investor's name to help protect them if the tenant decides to sue the landlord for any reason.

- **Purchase Methods.** One of the perks of buying a rental property is using fancy payment options like a 1031 Exchange (see the 1031 exchange chapter for more information) or fractional ownership. Explore these options first to get more from the property upfront and in the long term.

Bottom line—Do the homework, ask questions, and take as much time as you need. Once the deal is signed, though, and the cash flow begins, you'll wonder why you didn't do it sooner.

WHAT YOU SHOULD EXPECT IN A TURNKEY INVESTMENT

The phrase "turnkey investment" is bandied about quite freely in the real estate community. If you go on any of the universal real estate flip sites, you'll feel as if everyone and their brother has a supposed "turnkey investment opportunity" for you to buy. When you purchase a genuine turnkey investment, you should expect a lot more than you'll get from those other guys. A turnkey investment means something important to people I work with regularly. Here's what you should expect a turnkey company to take care of when you make a turnkey investment.

Choosing the Right Property

First, I make sure to get a very good price on all the properties I buy, so once the renovations are complete, the investors are left with a high return on investment. I acquire distressed properties from a variety of sources, including government listings, REO agents, private sellers, and more.

Conducting Extensive, Quality Renovations

After the acquisition, my expert contractors do a thorough inspection above and beyond what you'd get from an ordinary home inspector. They dig deep to make sure that they take care of every little thing that might be an issue. At that point, I use my skilled contractors to conduct extensive, quality renovations. They install new floors, trim, woodwork, doors, and windows. They replace the HVAC system, as well as the kitchen and bath fixtures. They even install new electrical wiring, rooftops, and drainage systems, as needed. That's the short of it.

Placing Quality, Screened Tenants

Of course, turnkey wouldn't be "turnkey" if my investors had to figure out how to rent out the properties they purchased. Managing tenant placement and turnover adds to the value of turnkey investment properties because the applicant criteria are very high. Income needs to be three times the rent, which automatically ensures that tenants earn in the higher figures and often means they are professionals with established careers. These types of applicants are much less likely to be susceptible to sudden job loss and subsequent inability to pay rent. Also, I check references, especially the previous landlord, if available, and meet the potential tenant in person. Official, complete background and credit checks must be in place before we offer a lease. These tenants are then signed to long-term leases to ensure cash flow and occupancy.

Providing Property Management Services

A true turnkey investment means you won't need to answer a call at 2 a.m. to fix a frozen pipe.

You won't hear from the local police about a noisy barking dog that isn't even supposed to be living on your rental property. You won't be forced to pester your tenant about their late rent check (that can be awkward).

Efficient property management companies handle the daily maintenance, such as raking leaves in the fall and changing out the water filter in the fridge, to those 2 a.m. calls, and all the paperwork. As an investor, you can trust management to reach out to you only when necessary. Most of the time, you can forget you even have an investment property—that is, until you see a nice chunk of change hit your bank account each month.

REAL ESTATE VS. THE STOCK MARKET

Deciding where to invest your money is hard, and there are pros and cons to putting your money in real estate vs. the stock market that goes beyond the annual returns. When you hear the word "invest," your mind might be conditioned to think "stock market." Although investing in the stock market is a perfectly viable way of making some side change, there is a better way. You already know what I'm going to say, and that's real estate investments.

The stock market is less predictable than the real estate market, and stocks are more likely to change more from day to day than property values. According to data pulled by the New York University Stern School of Business, the S&P 500 annual return landed at 1.38% in 2015 and then 21.64% in 2017, and that kind of fluctuation is not for the passive investor.

BENEFITS OF INVESTING IN REAL ESTATE VS. THE STOCK MARKET

The idea of investing in stocks is straightforward. You purchase a share with a company you think is doing well or heading in the right direction, watch the stock, and cash out whenever you want (preferably when it's riding high). In general, when you invest in the stock market, you are tied to the success (or failure) of the company in which you invest.

Real estate investors use many different strategies to generate a return on their investment. In the short term, investors buy homes, fix them up, and sell them, usually within sixty to ninety days, or before the market takes a seasonal turn. Other investors may buy properties and hold them for a long period while collecting passive income by renting those properties to other people. The following comparisons relate to the basic stock market buy-in and a passive real estate investment.

Let's look at the benefits of the stock market first.

- **Flexible Investments.** Stocks are easy to buy and easy to sell. Stocks are easy to liquidate or move to a retirement account tax-free until retirement.

- **Fluctuating Market.** The market is volatile, but it can produce returns as big as 20-50%. Now, let's consider the cons.

- **Fluctuating Market.** The volatile market that can work in your favor can also work against you. The fluctuations in the economy can negatively impact the performance of your stock portfolio, as much as -30% or more.

- **Risk of Bankruptcy**. If a company declares bankruptcy, your stake in the company essentially disappears. As a general shareholder, you typically don't have any right to the liquid value of the company. The possibility of bankruptcy should always be in the back of your mind.

- **Daily Check-ins.** You need to remain up to date with your stocks to anticipate a prime selling or trading time.

- **You vs. Brokers.** Some people do this for a living, working eighty hours a week watching stocks go up and down. There are large-scale companies dedicated to that task, and the individual stock market investor is a small fish in the middle of an endless ocean. Although it is possible to make money off the stock market, the method can require much more participation than you're able to give.

- **Associated Fees.** If you do decide to trade, you must consider fees. You will also have to pay (income) taxes on your stocks each year, including a capital gains tax if you've held onto them for more than a year.

I'm not saying you can't make money or even a lot of money from the stock market, but I am saying there's a better place to put your money. Let's talk about the pros of real estate investing.

- **High Potential Returns.** Although some high-value markets in the country have already reached their max potential within the current economy, those are few and far between when you compare the number of emerging markets. Investors who recognize the growth factors of a city or community know they can buy in at a reasonable, low price, and then sell two or ten years later for a substantially higher price. The same idea goes for the buy-and-hold option if the investor rents competitively. According to the BiggerPockets index for 2016, the area with the most favorable returns was Dallas, TX. Real estate investors in Dallas saw unleveraged returns of 20.7%.

- **Tax Benefits.** The many favorable tax benefits for real estate investors include deductions and depreciation. Also, a 1031 Exchange allows you to postpone paying capital gains if you use one to purchase your investment property.

- **Leverage.** In the stock market, $20,000 allows you to buy only $20,000 of stock, while in the real estate market, you can take that same $20K and pick up a $100,000 property. Leveraging an investment with a physical asset lends a feeling of security, too.

- **Predictable Market.** The buying season is typically in spring through early summer, and then the numbers drop off during colder months. The cycle repeats. Mortgage rates do fluctuate daily, but only by 0.01-0.03% on average.

- **Control.** You're the only person who owns your investment property. If you want to raise the rent price, then raise it. If you want to improve your investment by installing new appliances, do it. Property investments are truly unique to the investor.

CONS OF INVESTING IN REAL ESTATE

- **Challenging Liquidation.** Depending on the type of asset you purchase, it could be difficult to liquidate. As discussed earlier, when purchasing lower-priced single-family homes in primarily "renter occupied neighborhoods," your investment can be more difficult to sell. Retail homebuyers do not generally target these more distressed neighborhoods. It can also be difficult to sell a multi-family or commercial building(s) because these opportunities primarily trade on cap rate (return on investment) and not market value.

- **Slow Diversification.** When investing in real estate vs. the stock market, you'll need much longer to create a large diversified portfolio. Because each residential property requires a 20% down payment in addition to closing costs, growth and diversification can be slow.

- **Property Values Fluctuate.** There is always the risk of a fluctuating market. If you borrow too much or your closing costs are too high, you risk owing more than the property is worth, which would be an issue only if you made a not-so-great deal. For this reason, I recommend investing in markets with growing and diverse economies that will continue to drive population growth.

Many investors have seen excellent returns from the stock market. It is the traditional place to put your money to work for a reason! Or, you can take a different route by investing in real estate because of the passive income, tangibility, and potential for appreciation it provides. I encourage the idea of purchasing high-quality single-family rentals with reliable tenants in the properties and assigning a good property manager. Then, you can sit back and enjoy the cash flow without having to think about it.

THE DIFFERENCE BETWEEN A, B, AND C CLASS PROPERTIES

Investors, lenders, and brokers have developed property classifications to make it easier when communicating among themselves about the quality of the property. For investors, property class directly affects the projection of risk and return.

The grades on the properties are according to a combination of location and physical characteristics. Here are the factors considered:

- Age (original build year)
- Location
- Tenant income
- Area growth projections
- Appreciation or capital growth
- Amenities
- Rental income

Here's a breakdown.

Class A – These properties are the highest quality buildings in their market. They are new builds (usually built within the last twenty years), they come with high-end finishes that attract higher income-earning tenants and low vacancy rates. The crime rates are low, and the school district is top-notch. A professional company almost always manages Class A buildings and usually demands the highest rent with little or no deferred maintenance. Class A investments yield a more moderate rate of return on cash flow from rental income but can offer a higher overall rate of return through appreciation. If you are an investor looking for truly passive investment, I recommend going the Class A route.

Class B – In comparison to A, Class B properties are older and occupied by tenants with lower income. In some cases, these properties have professional management, but in my experience, not usually. Investors look at a Class B investment as an opportunity to add value through renovations and improvements. Sometimes, they can turn a B into an A; however, this is more of a hands-on approach for the investor and treated as a higher risk, less passive investment. Due to the higher risk involved with these types of properties, you are usually able to acquire Class Bs at a higher cap rate than Class As. Class B properties also come with less of an appreciation upside than Class A.

Class C – Class C properties are typically much older than twenty years and located in less desirable areas. Renovations are usually necessary. As a result, Class C buildings tend to have the lowest rental rates in the market. They also have the highest rate of vacancy, late or missed rental payments, and deferred maintenance, all of which negatively affect cash flow. They're not ideal for an investor who expects a passive investment. These investments are very "hands on." Truly professional management companies with the proper infrastructure in place rarely manage these types of investments. Class C investments typically offer a higher return on rental income but based on the elevated risk, higher returns are tough to achieve and maintain. Class C properties also come with little-to-no appreciation upside when not positioned in areas that are attractive to retail home buyers. These properties trade from investor to investor and the cap rate determines the transaction rather than market value. Although the potential return looks attractive on paper, it is very difficult to see that type of return year-over-year with Class C investments. Remember, you are purchasing a home not a piece of paper or spreadsheet.

Investors use the differences in property class types to consider how each property fits within their investment strategy. This strategy bases itself on return objectives and the amount of risk they are willing to accept to achieve those returns.

Depending on what you are looking for as an investor, you need to identify that and match it with the correct property class. For those looking for capital preservation and appreciation in their market, I recommend a Class A investment.

DETAILED BENEFITS OF CLASS A REAL ESTATE INVESTMENTS
Class A real estate has more upfront costs than other classes; however, the benefits of Class A property investments vastly outweigh the others.

Safety
Class A real estate is in neighborhoods with low crime rates. You'll never have to worry about your safety when visiting the property for any reason. Safety is a top priority for many high-end renters, especially families. In conjunction with safety comes a sense of community, one that is well served by public infrastructures such as emergency services and neighborhood surveillance.

Higher Rents
Class A properties naturally demand higher rents. They are in desirable neighborhoods, where professionals with high incomes reside. The neighborhoods with Class A real estate are largely owner-occupied, which is where high-income renters also want to live. For example, in the Dallas-Fort Worth (DFW) area, where the economy is thriving with new job creation, investors can increase rents annually. So, not only could you charge a higher rent to start with, but should you decide to increase rent annually, you would be consistent with market conditions.

Stability
The types of higher income tenants who are attracted to Class A real estate are engaged in stable, professional careers. When a tenant maintains employment, the investor maintains cash flow. Another aspect of stability is the long-term commitment of the tenant. Investors

don't want to think about vacancy or turnovers.

Better Prospects for Investment Return

With an investment in Class A real estate, there is always a huge likelihood that you'll be able to get a nice return on your initial investment. With Fortune 500 companies moving into desirable areas like DFW, the demand for quality rental homes is high. That drives up both rent and property values. Over time, when your tenant has paid down your interest and principal, you could leverage your investment, opt to take out the equity, and buy a second investment.

LIFESTYLE INVESTING THROUGH VACATION RENTAL PROPERTIES

When people take off for vacation, they're often heading somewhere warm where they can relax. They run to the beach, wedge a chair in the sand, and turn off their phones as someone walks up with a cold Mai Tai. Spring break, summer vacations, weekend getaways—you name it—people keep coming back to the beaches of paradise.

Exotic, yet simple and accessible, Belize was much like mid-century Hawaii. While saturation of tourists on the East Coast and Florida increased, Hawaii slowly pulled people in with its raw beauty and serene way of life. Through the decades, it maintains its simplistic roots and is still a much sought-after destination, making long-standing vacation rental properties rare gems.

Wouldn't it be amazing to go back in time and take a chance on a beachfront lot in Hawaii, knowing what it is worth today? I'm telling you right now that you still have that chance—in Belize.

Belize is a paradise with its white sand beaches, tropical climate, adventure on land and sea, intense beauty, and vast accessibility. People not only want to vacation there, but they dream of owning property there, whether a beachfront condo or an entire private island. Investors can fly south and relax in their properties anytime, and they also can make a profit without even being in the country.

Year after year, the property appreciates. More people begin to feel the draw of Belize R&R. Tourism rates push the rental prices up and improve property value. Suddenly, the investor who took a risk is sitting on one of those rare gems.

GETTING STARTED AS AN INVESTOR IN BELIZE

In the case of international investments, the term "passive" is more important than ever. A vacation rental property, for instance, should be completely up to date with modern amenities, stylishly furnished, well maintained, and situated in a desirable location. All those features attract top-paying renters. Obtaining such an investment property seems like it would cost a fortune, and then there's the question of finding a reputable property management company. What if I told you that you could buy such a property (with a fully equipped management team) for literally a fraction of the cost?

Fractional ownership is what the name describes. It's an ownership structure where several people agree to share in the costs, risks, usage, and returns of an asset (in our case, luxury vacation homes in Belize) to reap the benefits of something that may have been too cost-prohibitive or time-intensive to purchase. In the case of a vacation home, several benefits of fractional ownership make it very different from a timeshare and very attractive to buyers.

REASONS FOR FRACTIONAL OWNERSHIP

Fractional ownership is a straightforward model for buying vacation homes. Its benefits are enough to motivate many potential vacation homeowners to take the plunge and buy a property. Here's why.

Reason #1. Fractional Ownership Is More Affordable

Would you rather buy a beach house for $150,000 or $1,500,000? It probably depends on the house, right? Well, what if you could buy a $1,500,000 beach home for $150,000? That's how fractional ownership works. For $150,000, you can buy 10% ownership in a luxury beach home worth $1,500,000. Then consider the fact that property values will rise consistently over the next five to ten years.

Reason #2. Fractional Ownership Spreads the Costs Around

Routine costs of cleaning, repairs, taxes, and property management decline when split ten ways. In addition, a newly built or renovated vacation home can limit these extra costs in the first few years of ownership.

Reason #3. Fractional Ownership Is Worry-Free

When owners aren't there to watch the house 24/7, they need to have a trusted, qualified team onsite. Property management is especially important when the vacation home is in another country. Here's what you can expect from one:

- Daily cleaning
- Addressing service needs for guests
- Handling emergencies
- Taking on repairs
- Alerting owners of property condition
- Managing bookings and communicating with guests
- Making payments for insurance, taxes, utilities
- Tracking finances

Of course, the duties of a property management company can vary, but having a strong team in place makes it easier to own a vacation home.

Reason #4. Fractional Ownership Is Real Ownership

When purchasing a timeshare, the buyer usually acquires the right to use a property, but they don't obtain any physical ownership of the property. With fractional ownership, the buyer acquires real assets—the land, the structure, the furniture. Owners also have the right to make decisions on matters regarding the property.

Reason #5. Fractional Ownership Offers A Real Exit Strategy

Fractional ownership shares can be bought and sold like any piece of real estate, at any time. No mortgage payments are involved either. The share is owned outright by each owner, so there is no risk of default.

Reason #6. Fractional Ownership Has Its Perks

Our company has developed partnerships with groups like THIRDHOME to give our fractional owners access to other vacation properties around the world. So, even though the owner has a property in Belize, he or she can vacation in places like Cabo San Lucas, Vail, France, Amsterdam, Dubai, and many more.

Reason #7. Fractional Ownership Turns A Profit

Many fractional owners decide to use their share(s) as an investment. With their share, the owner has access to the vacation home for five weeks every year. If this owner chooses to rent out all five weeks rather than use them personally, they can generate passive income after their share of expenses are paid on the home. Not too shabby!

Reason #8. Fractional Ownership Is All About Luxury

The property should show well and have the "wow factor" that makes renters feel they're getting a truly luxurious experience. The property caretakers—from a full-time chef to private transportation—also play a pivotal role in making luxury come to life.

Reason #9. Fractional Ownership Includes Private Island Ownership

Owning a private island is the epitome of a luxury real estate investment, and it's within reach through fractional ownership. These properties are truly private and always unique. With a good management team in place and co-owners to split the costs and mitigate the risk, it's too perfect to pass up. Check out this amazing private island built for HGTV star, Chris Krolow. It's called Gladden Caye.

Why Not Consider Fractional Ownership?

Fractional ownership is a good option for vacation home buyers who want to own luxury real estate for a fraction of the cost. It's an ideal investment for someone who wants a place to occasionally vacation without being tied down to only one home or one location forever. Fractional ownership is for the person who wants real ownership, not just the right to vacation somewhere on occasion. And finally, fractional ownership is perfect for the investor looking for a non-traditional asset. Vacation properties in Belize currently offer a great return on investment at an affordable price. Fractional ownership is a modern alternative to buying a dream vacation home.

7 THINGS TO CONSIDER WHEN INVESTING IN CASH FLOW PROPERTIES

You're ready to dive into real estate and reap the benefits of a passive investment. But before you can enjoy the cash flow, you need to do a bit of homework. You'll find it extremely worthwhile to take the time to sort through the following considerations, so you make sure to nail it the first time.

1. Appreciation/Capital Growth in Your Market

Look for markets with high population growth as this drives up the price of real estate in any market because of high demand and low inventory. Always look for job growth in the cities in which you are looking to invest. Research the Fortune 500 companies that are moving into your target market and bringing an abundance of jobs with them. As more people move into the area, the real estate market begins to adjust. This adjustment can take a few years. As an investor, you want to be part of the market from the get-go, so your investment can blossom alongside market growth.

2. Cash Flow

Cash flow is important, but do not be fooled by "paper yields." A paper yield is something that looks profitable on paper but is a high-risk, high-reward scenario. Lower grade properties in more distressed areas typically offer a higher return on investment but do not always perform as expected. Such properties also have less room for capital growth. The distressed areas I'm talking about are in and around the major inner cities across the United States. Higher grade properties in superior areas/neighborhoods, with better school districts, provide a smaller return but are consistently safer assets to own. These properties have locations in the suburbs outside of the inner city. They attract a higher quality tenant and tend to show higher appreciation and capital growth. Although they may not provide high cash flow numbers, remember that low-grade properties have higher risks and higher paper yields. On the other hand, high-grade properties have low risks and consistent returns. If you are not losing money each month, you are winning if you invest in the right market.

3. Tenant Profile

The tenant profile consideration is simple. Lower grade properties attract a less reliable tenant regarding meeting rent obligations, whereas high-grade properties in better areas/neighborhoods attract reliable tenants who can commit long-term. Remember, when you are purchasing an income-producing property, you are also purchasing the type of tenant this property will attract. In less affluent neighborhoods, petty crime rates (for break-ins, theft, vandalism, and so forth) are higher, and properties become subject to a higher probability of such crimes. No one wants to live in an area with higher crime rates, but sometimes being able to afford anything else is out of the question. People who are stuck in a paycheck-to-paycheck cycle are likely living in these neighborhoods and could easily slip into rent delinquency, move out of the property without notifying anyone, or cause unusual wear and tear on the home. It's more common for low-grade properties to have multiple tenants in one unit. One bad tenant can easily swallow up an entire year's worth of cash flow from missed rent payments, vacancy due to constant tenant turnover, or tenant-induced damage to the property. You MUST consider this when investing in a managed, cash flow asset.

4. Vacancy

Property vacancy is an assumption you should always consider when calculating your return on investment. When investing in a lower grade asset, you should make sure to account a larger portion of your net income to the vacancy because you must pay for an empty unit or spend money to rehab the unit to make it livable for the next person. Research shows that properties in more distressed markets produce a higher rate of vacancy because of many factors, including tenant income.

Look at Section 8 tenants, for example. They are not paying out-of-pocket to live in the home and have no financial liability (such as a security deposit) associated with the property, and they are more likely to vacate at their own will. Statistics show that tenants who rent lower grade properties in more distressed markets occupy the property for six to twelve months on average. The low occupancy timeframe is primarily due to eviction for non-payment of rent or breaking the parameters of the lease.

As I stated before, properties located in more stable areas/neighborhoods that rent for higher prices produce a more reliable tenant. This type of tenant has a higher paying job and brings in a larger sum of household income. In most cases, these tenants take better care of the dwelling because they are concerned with getting their security deposit back. Not all people who rent in better neighborhoods are exceptional tenants; however, buying in those neighborhoods certainly does mitigate the risk for early departure or eviction.

5. Rehab Quality/Maintenance

Make sure you are purchasing an investment property that has gone through a quality renovation and has been inspected by a third-party inspection company because this is extremely important when calculating your return. A property that has undergone a total renovation and has passed a third-party inspection should cost you little to nothing in maintenance expenses (especially in your first year of ownership). Ask for tax abatements as well. Most legitimate turnkey property providers will issue you a ninety-day to one-year warranty if they have done a full renovation and stood by their work. Be wary of the companies who will not stand by their work and avoid warranties because this usually means they have cut corners on their rehabs and are not providing their clients with a true, fully renovated, turnkey asset.

Pay attention to the estimated life left on the roof and all mechanicals (A/C, furnace, and hot water tank). You should avoid purchasing a home with a roof that has fewer than five years of life remaining. Ideally, you want your roof and mechanicals to have at least five to ten years left. I have found that this is a good benchmark that can help avoid costly repairs in the short-term.

6. Property Management

Property management is the greatest factor in keeping an investment performing at its highest potential. As an investor, your property manager should be your eyes and ears on the ground. A good property manager watches over your investment as if it is their own. It is not uncommon for a knowledgeable investor to interview two or three different management companies before making a final decision on who should be responsible for their asset. I have seen many investments fail because of poor management.

When searching for a property manager, you want to answer these key concerns.

a) How many homes do they manage?

b) How many property managers (PM) do they employ, and how many homes do they allocate to each PM? I have found a safe number is approximately 200-250 units. I believe this number is the industry average. If a PM is saturated, they are probably not giving each property, tenant, and owner the necessary attention they deserve.

c) What type of infrastructure do they have in place? You want a PM who has departments in place for different aspects of the business (leasing, marketing, maintenance, utilities, customer service, insurance, *etc.*) to ensure better follow-up and handling.

d) What type of properties do they manage? Ask for a description of an average property they currently have under management. There are many property management companies out there that specialize in different types of properties (single-family, multi-family, and commercial). Many property management companies also have certain criteria by which they abide. For example, some companies will only manage properties that rent for $1,000 per month and above. Some specialize in managing lower grade assets in more distressed inner-city areas. Just be sure that whatever type of property you invest in, you do your homework and match it with the right management company.

e) Does your PM have an online system in place? In today's world, we all want information fast. We like to track our packages to see when they arrive; we like to keep track of our banking information on our phones. Why wouldn't we want to keep track of our investment on our smartphone or personal computer as well? Almost all the great property management companies I have worked with over the years have an online portal set up for their owners and tenants, and this is the place where owners can track rental payments and maintenance requests, and on the flip side, it's a place where tenants can submit maintenance requests and pay rent. Tracking software or methods help to keep everyone accountable and on the same page.

7. Exit Strategy

When investing in any real estate, you should already have an idea of an exit strategy from the very beginning. As an investor, what are you trying to get out of this property? Are you looking for long-term cash flow by building a portfolio? Or are you seeking an investment in an appreciating market that you can hold for a short period, and then sell in three to five years to cash in on the capital gains? Whatever it is, you need to have a plan. If you execute it correctly, you should be well on your way to becoming a successful real estate investor.

PRIVATE MONEY LENDING: BE THE BANK

Most real estate exchanges involve a lender and a borrower. The party with the least amount of risk involved is almost always the lender. Before the lender even agrees to take pen to paper, he or she will go down a long checklist of objectives to ensure the deal is in his or her favor. On the other end, the borrower must play by the lender's rules.

As an investor, you have other options. Private money lending offers you the opportunity to be extremely risk-averse when passively investing in real estate opportunities. Private money lending has become a very attractive investment option for people looking to diversify because they can utilize their personal IRA or 401(k). As much as people are conditioned to leave those accounts alone until retirement, the money is still yours. You can, in fact, take a good chunk of change out as long as you pay it back within a certain time. If you want to borrow from yourself via your retirement fund, the first step is to set up a self-directed account. It's a separate account into which you can move funds from your 401(k) or an IRA. Such an account needs to be specially monitored and protected, so you'll need to go through an equity trust company or specific bank. At that point, you can take control of your retirement funds and diversify into other investment options like private lending. This option is quickly picking up speed because the funds return to the account tax-free or tax-deferred, a term all investors like to hear.

Is this Option for You?

If you're reading this, it's very likely that you've had a say in how you built your 401(k). Perhaps you've aggressively contributed to it over the years or agreed to have your company match your input. If you're tucking away more than 15% of your annual income into your 401(k), it should be looking ripe. Now, look at your bank account. Do you have funds sitting stagnant in an IRA or CD? You can dip into those accounts as well.

Ideally, you want to be able to lend money and allow that loan to mature. If you're under a time constraint and need that capital returned to you before the loan maturity date, you may end up trapped. In private lending ventures, lend only amounts you can part with for 1-5 to years while receiving interest payments.

Taking on Risks

Once you know how much money you want to invest and where it's coming from it's time to calculate the risks. The most critical component to private lending is the creation of a plan A, B, and C for the borrower to pay back the loan. For instance, some private lending options can yield up to 15% returns or greater on your money, which is very attractive; however, the risks are probably high. If you're working with a borrower, and he or she is willing to pay you a higher interest payment for a loan, be aware. The borrower may be more desperate for the money because he or she is running a project that comes with great risk. Also, note that private lenders are good options for borrowers who might not pass the "numbers test" with a bank, so you'll have to perform your due diligence before striking a deal.

As a private lender, you have your trust deed to protect you, and with that, you will be the owner of the project. If the borrower defaults, you will still have to deal with a costly foreclosure process, and you may end up owing on a project that is difficult to liquidate. Again, do your due diligence and vet out any project and borrower when getting into private lending, which means hitting the pavement and physically checking out properties and projects yourself. Sometimes, taking a more moderate rate of return on a safer project can be a better option to ensure the return of your principal. With that caveat, it's best to utilize private lending in moderate- to low-risk investments, especially if you're getting your feet wet.

Repeat borrowers are excellent assets for private lenders. You can establish a working relationship and credit history that can add to your bottom line. Another benefit of finding a good group to lend to is the potential for future investment opportunities. By working with the same borrower or commercial broker to secure your loans, you can continue to roll your initial capital investment into other projects as you receive payments. This way, you can continue to get your money to work for you even more efficiently.

INVESTING IN REAL ESTATE WITH YOUR RETIREMENT FUNDS

You don't have to wait until retirement to access the money in your retirement accounts. Of course, the entire concept of such an account is to set yourself up for a comfortable life after you punch your last timecard. But it's still your money, and you can move it into a viable investment opportunity to make it worth even more.

As we already discussed, most 401(k) plans allow you to borrow from your account before retirement, but the rules are strict. You can borrow $50,000 or up to 50%, whichever is less, and you can only do so every twelve months. Repayment is typically a withdrawal from your paycheck over the span of no more than five years. The interest rate on the repayment is low, but guess what? You're paying interest to yourself. Let's say you can't pay it back because you lost your job or pulled the funds for something frivolous, not an investment, and lose cash flow. When you fail to repay, the IRS classifies this as an early distribution and will slap you with taxes. But because you're using the funds for an investment property that will churn out an 8% to 12% return, you'll be fine.

Prep Your 401(k) or IRA for Borrowing

The average American contributes about 6% of each paycheck to a 401(k) plan. The investor should contribute closer to 15% for a robust account. That money is coming to you one way or another, so wouldn't it make more sense to put it into a tax-sheltered account versus a diluted amount into your pocket?

If you opted for an IRA instead, or have one in addition to your 401(k), those funds are also available to you at any time. The deal for borrowing from an IRA is much stricter and comes with a shorter lifespan. You are required to pay it back into the account within 60 days. With that said, the gains from your investment will pour back into your IRA tax-free. Remember, IRA funds come from taxed income, so every cent that goes into your IRA remains in your possession.

Don't have an IRA? It's easy to set up. Choose a provider, fill out a form with your name and social security number on it, and then fund the account.

Retirement Funds vs. Personal Funds

The money sitting in your 401(k) or IRA is yours. When it comes to acquiring investment properties, you need a liquid asset, at least for the down payment. You can dip into your retirement accounts and pull out $20,000 for a $100,000 property that rents for $800 a month right away. If you use non-retirement funds for the investment, the $20,000 is absorbed completely into the property unlike if you use your 401(k), and the $20,000 is coming back to you (with interest). Once the loan is repaid (to yourself), you have $800 a month in the present plus $20,000 with interest after age 59½.

Tips for Investing

Your success lies in the details. The ability to pay the borrowed amount back in full by the deadline is not so much a detail but a key component for success. Everything else, like how much to borrow, when, whether to set up an IRA or IRA LLC, which property to purchase, whose name goes on it, and more is all subject to your skill as an investor. To get you started on the right foot, here are a few things to consider.

- Your retirement funds must not go under your name. Instead, once the funds are withdrawn from the account and placed into your investment account, the 401(k) provider or an IRA LLC or trust company holds the name. Otherwise, they would look like personal funds.

- If you make a down payment but require financing for the rest, opt for a nonrecourse loan that ties the money to the property instead of the person (borrower).

- Set up your accounts in the state where you are purchasing your property.

- Look for ready-to-go properties that do not require work before renting out; using vacation properties for business is ideal, but not your summerhouse on the beach.

- Be a diligent record-keeper. All transactions, receipts, paperwork should be copied and on hand.

- Talk with a tax expert to review your funds and specific possibilities.

Dipping into your retirement funds to invest does come with risk, as any investment does. The process requires strict adherence to a plan, but once that's locked down, you'll be able to experience an above-average return on your accounts. Also, you can set yourself up to receive added cash flow each year with a primed investment property—a property you would have had to pass up if you didn't play your 401(k) card.

5 MISTAKES REAL ESTATE INVESTORS MAKE

New real estate investors often see the industry as a chance to fill their pockets quickly and easily. But as many experienced investors know, it's not as cut and dry as it may look from the outside. As is the case with any investment strategy, you must keep a few critical things in mind when starting out. If you ignore these important steps in the beginning, you may end up with much unnecessary pain down the road.

According to Webster's dictionary, due diligence is "the care that a prudent person might be expected to exercise in the examination and evaluation of risks affecting a business transaction." Due diligence is the key that separates a successful real estate investor from a failed investor. When it comes to due diligence in real estate, here are five areas where you should pay attention.

1) Know Your Market

Is the property located in a good neighborhood with low crime rates and highly rated schools? Is it near an airport or located across the street from the city dump? How do the comps look for the property? What's the average time on the market of properties for sale versus for rent? Every investor should have an intimate knowledge of the market where they plan to invest. At the very least, the investor should have a trusted advisor who already knows the market extremely well.

2) Know Your Goals

What is motivating you to invest in real estate? The answer to this question should affect where and how you choose to invest. Are you looking for long-term, passive income investments? If so, you probably want to invest in properties that offer good appreciation, low maintenance, and are in quality neighborhoods. Are you trying to replace your current income with new streams of cash flow? If so, your strategy may lie in lower cost, higher return assets.

3) To Flip or Not to Flip

If you know what you're doing when it comes to rehabbing a house, then a fix-and-flip strategy might be right for you. But if you have no experience in rehabbing homes, then you may want to avoid the fix-and-flip strategy altogether. If you've decided to flip a house, then you should hire a professional contractor or a trusted advisor to provide a true estimate of the rehab costs required for the house-flip. That information must be on hand before you make an offer. In addition to a plan on paper, go ahead and gain approval for a construction loan and line up permits. Making estimates about rehab costs that you don't understand often results in money lost for a first-time investor, even if you can resell the property for more. Flips can be total flops.

4) Paper Yield

If the fix-and-flip strategy isn't part of your plan, then you're probably looking for cash flow real estate. But be careful. There is more to cash flowing real estate than just the numbers on paper.

New real estate investors often get fooled by what is called a "paper yield," or something that looks profitable on paper but is a high-risk, high-reward scenario.

Here's an example of a paper yield:

- Property Value = $77,000
- Monthly Rent = $900
- Taxes = $950
- Insurance = $600
- Management Fee = 8%
- Est. Net Return = 10-11%

Sounds like a pretty good investment, right? Properties like the one in the example above are in more distressed areas of the country. Rental rates may be lower, but tenant profiles are also less favorable, resulting in higher late payment and eviction rates. With this type of property, you may have a chance at a higher return, but you also increase your investment's risk profile. While this isn't a bad investment, the investor needs to decide how much risk to take.

5) Quality Property Management

Property management is by far the most time-consuming piece of real estate investing. A property rehab may only take a few months, but managing a property is a never-ending task. It starts with identifying quality tenants who will take care of the property and pay rent consistently. Then, it evolves into maintenance and repairs, and it eventually returns to finding a new tenant and starting over again. For most real estate investors, quality property management is difficult to achieve on their own. Quality tenants take time to identify, and ongoing maintenance of property requires personal time or trust in a contractor to do good work.

Professional property management companies are a good solution for the hands-off investor, but it's important to find a company with the appropriate infrastructure in place to manage a high volume of homes.

Turning to Turnkey Investments

If you decide that passive real estate investing is your strategy, then turnkey investments may be your best option. Genuinely "turnkey" means that there is very little work for the investor. Maintaining the property is almost as simple as walking to your mailbox and collecting your check each month. Nothing is ever quite that simple, but the problems of a turnkey investor are usually few and far between. That's why turnkey real estate investments are the choice for many.

WHAT I WISH EVERY INVESTOR KNEW ABOUT TURNKEY REAL ESTATE INVESTMENTS

Turnkey real estate companies are everywhere. You can probably find one in every major city of the United States. However, not all turnkey real estate companies are the same, and it can be difficult to identify the good ones unless you have an idea of what to expect. As I mentioned earlier, anyone can slap a coat of paint on the property, take some compelling before and after photos, pick a tenant out of a hat, and advertise as a turnkey investor. But is this the type of turnkey real estate company you want to put in charge of your money? Before you take the plunge and purchase your first turnkey investment property, take my advice and learn what I wish every investor knew about the industry.

With Turnkey Real Estate, Consider the Market and the Property

When you purchase a turnkey real estate property, you're not just investing in the home. You are also buying into the local market. Consider the answers to specific questions.

- What are the vacancy rates in the area?

- Who is renting here?

- Are the homes appreciating in value?

Forbes consistently ranks Dallas as the top (or top few) real estate investment markets and industry experts rank Texas as the top state for business (2018). When building their list, Forbes looked at some key indicators that could assist you in your due diligence of a market:

Real Estate Key Indicators

Although there is no way to accurately predict the future growth or decline of a real estate market, you can still benefit by doing some research on just a few of the markets where you are considering investing.

- Past and Projected Job Growth

- Cost of Living

- Income Growth

- Projected Economic Growth

Consider the Location

Even in a thriving market like Dallas, home values and property classifications can vary from neighborhood to neighborhood. When looking at potential investment properties, think about some of your criteria for buying a home:

- What are the neighborhood demographics?
- How are the schools?
- What amenities are available nearby?

Quality neighborhoods not only attract quality tenants, but the homes in these areas are more likely to hold or even increase in value. Take a step back before deciding on your investment to ensure that you choose a property that will attract quality tenants.

Ask About Renovation Quality

When you purchase a turnkey investment property in a quality market and quality neighborhood, your tenants expect a quality home. Before purchasing a turnkey real estate property, ask the provider about the renovation. Focus on the large expenses like the roof, HVAC, and water heater.

Just about anyone can be dazzled by before and after photos. Some paint and HDR photography can give the illusion that the property you are purchasing is in pristine condition. So, ask the important questions and make sure the turnkey provider offers a warranty on all repairs that they made, minor and major. You don't want to be a turnkey real estate investor who constantly spends time and money on repairs.

Profits and Property Management

Investing in real estate is, after all, an investment, so seeing a financial return is the bottom line. The profits you see each month depend on a variety of factors, including successful tenant placement. When you purchase a property from a true turnkey real estate provider that also offers property management, you are more likely to have a quality tenant placed in your home. The success of a property management company and a turnkey provider rests as much on the quality of the tenant as it does on the quality of the property.

Working with a professional property management company will help you avoid costly situations.

Let Property Management Handle These:
- Evictions
- Tenant Damages

- Vacancy
- Late or Unpaid Rent
- Turnovers
- Tenant Complaints
- Maintenance Requests
- Specialty Repair Estimates

You can profit from real estate while outsourcing your property management. Be sure you understand the monthly expenses of working with a property management company.

Find a Genuine Turnkey Real Estate Provider

With all I've mentioned here, you are probably thinking about the work that must be done upfront before the cash flow can begin. It doesn't matter if you're a first-timer or a veteran investor—you no doubt would like to have someone do all this work for you. That's the role of a turnkey real estate provider. It's typically a company of experienced professionals within the industry who gather all the data, select prime properties, grow them into cash-flowing machines, and hand them off to investors like you. Here's what you can expect from a provider:

- Guidance on property searching
- Assistance with the closing process
- Recommendations on property management services
- Regular updates on your property
- Support for any issues with your investment

Find a turnkey partner who will be there every step of the way, before, during and after the ink is dry.

Even if you purchase a quality home, in an excellent market, you may still leave money on the table if you don't have a good team to support your investment.

THE POWER OF THE 1031 EXCHANGE

A 1031 exchange is your property investment unicorn, a deal so sweet that it is frequently used but largely regulated. If you take advantage of a 1031 exchange once, there's a high likelihood you'll do it again and again. It's that amazing.

A 1031 exchange is a government-regulated transaction, which means that you are working with the IRS. Whenever the IRS is involved, you must have proper documentation and realistic timelines. The idea of a 1031 exchange is to swap one investment property for another (or "like kind") within a specific timeframe. This real estate swap allows you to avoid paying Uncle Sam any capital gains taxes on your transaction.

How a 1031 Exchange Works to Your Benefit

Let's say you own a rental property, but the return on investment has plateaued. You're bored and want to explore more lucrative real estate investments. In a case like this, you can utilize a 1031 exchange to continue earning passive income, decrease your losses, and acquire better appreciating assets.

Ideally, you can locate your desired property and swap out your unwanted property in the same deal. The more common route, though, is to sell your current property, put your profits into a holding account, locate your next property (or properties), and close the deal within 180 days of your former property's sale. At the end of the process, you have a new investment property, hopefully, loaded with earning potential, and you didn't have to dilute your portfolio. To be clear, everything you made off property A can roll into the down payment of property B.

What if, in another scenario, your investment profits outweigh the 20 to 25% down payment you would make with a new investment? Can you keep some of your money? In short, yes. However, whatever you keep from your initial sale will be taxed. It's nice to have options, however.

7 Things to Know About a 1031 Exchange

1. It applies only to like-kind properties, and you can't swap personal property or personal residences (including vacation homes). You can, however, swap rental housing for land and vice versa, if the land is in use for business. The single-family home rental market is ideal for this type of exchange.

2. A 1031 exchange is tax-deferred, not tax-free. Don't be swindled by anyone who tells you otherwise.

3. You need to identify as a business in this transaction. Instead of John Smith, do a little extra paperwork to become John Smith, LLC or sign as your business.

4. If you're not going to swap, you can do a deferred exchange. You have forty-five days to close on the sale of your property. You have 180 days to close on your new property, beginning from the close of your first sale. Be careful about selling your property late in the year (such as in December). According to the IRS, there is a restriction on your 180-day exchange period according to the due date of your income tax return for the year property A sold. You can always file for an extension, but this restriction can potentially cause problems.

5. Reverse exchanges are also possible. They involve acquiring your desired property first, putting it into an exchange accommodation titleholder, and then selling your unwanted property within 180 days.

6. You cannot hold onto your profits during the 180-day exchange period of a 1031 exchange. You'll need to find a highly reputable intermediary or exchange facilitator to do this for you.

7. Be prepared to cross your T's and dot your I's at the end of the tax year by submitting Form 8824.

The Time is Now for A 1031 Exchange

There is some talk of the government cutting Section 1031 and replacing it with something potentially more beneficial to real estate investors. Right now, it's just speculation, but eliminating this policy would change the landscape of real estate transactions. Either way you swing it, we're at the height of a seller's market, and the 1031 exchange is a valuable tool for investors. Your window of opportunity is right now.

EVERYTHING YOU SHOULD CONSIDER ABOUT PROPERTY MANAGEMENT

Rental properties are an excellent source of income. But like any investment, a rental property comes with a certain level of attention and care. For rental property owners, it's sometimes best to hand over the responsibility to a reputable property management company. Before deciding on one, let's look at the basics of what's involved in managing a rental property.

BASICS OF PROPERTY MANAGEMENT

Property

First, consider the type of property and the location. Is it a single-family home, a duplex, or an apartment? Is the unit located in the city, the suburbs, or a rural area? Is it only one unit or multiple units? A multi-unit building in the city will require more work for the manager, but the work may be more efficient than an investment of multiple SFR properties scattered throughout a large metro area. Too many homes can be a juggling act for a part-time property manager.

Tenants

Property management also includes finding, screening, and managing quality tenants. The property manager communicates directly with the tenants on a day-to-day or week-to-week basis. Property owners who choose to manage the property need to make smart decisions early on about who lives there, so the management is low-scale.

Maintenance

One of the most important aspects of property management is the maintenance of the property. Maintenance can range from weekly lawn cutting, repairing a dishwasher, to finding a contractor to replace the roof or water heater. The list of ongoing maintenance is long and extensive, especially once you've owned a property for many years.

Deciding to Manage a Property

In real estate investing, location is everything. The same idea goes for property management. It's best to hand off management of your property to a local company if your rental property isn't local to you—let's say more than one hour away. Property management requires proactive care, not reactive. Staying on top of minor repairs can limit the potential for costly repairs in the future. A property owner should be able to drive past the rental once a week to make sure tenants haven't left bulk trash items on the curb, for example, or to check for any damage from a recent storm.

Must-haves

Here are a few other items to consider when trying to decide if you should manage your properties or hand off the job to a property management company.

- Accessibility. Is the PM able to get to the property promptly if an emergency arises? Is he or she comfortable being "on-call" when a tenant needs something?

- Legal matters. Is the manager equipped to draft a lease that will protect the investor, protect the assets, and follow tenant protection laws? A manager must be willing to communicate with the tenant and follow through with tough decisions without emotion.

- Network. A manager needs to be able to call in a plumber when water backs into the tub and feel confident that the cost is fair and the work is good. Be prepared to manage a trustworthy network of vendors.

Tenant Turnovers

Aside from the daily or weekly tasks, a manager handles tenant selection, and this can quickly become a frustrating process if not managed correctly. Management involves knowing the market and finding the right tenant for a property.

Here's what the process of turning over a unit usually looks like:

1. Receive notification of leave from the current tenant (30-45 days)
2. Access the property; create postings and marketing materials
3. Screen interested renters via phone or email
4. Set up showings (individual or open-house style)
5. Prepare an application; screen accordingly by checking references
6. Process credit and criminal background checks on highest priority applicants
7. Create lease; set time for walk-through and lease signing
8. Check property when current tenant leaves; assess damage, and then prep for a new tenant
9. Set up rent collection and obtain the security deposit

Find Your Best Tenants

An ideal tenant is one who pays on time, keeps the property clean, communicates important matters right away, is flexible with repair work, easy to reach, and causes minimal wear on the property. They also have a decent credit score and excellent references.

> *Tip:* *Your best bet for finding an excellent tenant is to check his or her references. If possible, ask for the previous landlord's contact information. The applicant's current landlord might say anything to get the tenant out of their place, but a previous landlord (or employer) will always be honest.*

Ongoing Property Management

With a quality tenant in place, it's easier to relax, especially if there's a professional property manager at work. Most property management companies take care of minor maintenance requests without bothering the property owner. And a good PM provides regular, detailed monthly updates. For a real estate investment to be protected when you, the investor, cannot be present, you must have a team that treats the property as their own.

> *"As a company philosophy, we decided we didn't want to put too much on any property manager's plate," explains Kyle Karker from American Real PM. "At the end of the day, it's all about relationships, and it's about people. We need to be constantly able to build relationships with people."*

Property management is a job done in real-time with complete knowledge of what every property needs. Excellent communication and accessibility with property managers are non-negotiable for owners.

Scotty Mitchell, co-founder, and COO of American Real PM explains:

> *"What sets us apart, is that we stay focused on the investor, and our values and goals align with the investor's values and goals. We also employ best practices of 24-hour communication and 24-hour response. Our policy is that within 24 hours, it doesn't matter how you communicate with us, even if we don't have the answer yet, we'll respond [to you]."*

Mitchell notes that an experienced manager knows when an issue requires a contractor and when it doesn't. No owner wants to spend $100 on a service call for a water filter replacement. An investor should feel confident that a property manager can do the legwork of troubleshooting maintenance requests, taking bids, and coming up with a game plan when problems arise.

A rental property can be a sweet deal with a trustworthy property management system in place.

SUCCESSFUL HABITS OF TOP REAL ESTATE INVESTORS

There is no such thing as a risk-free investment. But as far as sound investments go, real estate is as good a choice as any. The stock market may be the go-to investment for many, but top real estate investors see rental properties as a more favorable alternative because of benefits like better returns, tax perks, and leverage.

"Real estate investors get paid five ways simultaneously," says Get Rich Education Founder and real estate investor Keith Weinhold. "Stocks only pay you one way, sometimes two."

How Top Real Estate Investors Get Ahead

You need more than just a checkbook to make a profit and succeed as a real estate investor, however. You also need discipline, research, and good habits that are put into practice every time you make a real estate investment.

The good news is you don't have to reinvent the proverbial real estate investor wheel to be successful. Many investors have succeeded in this field. And if you follow their patterns, there is no reason you cannot find success. Heck, maybe people will soon study about you to find out what made you a successful real estate investor!

Here are just a few successful habits of top real estate investors.

1) Continuing Education

Top real estate investors understand the importance of a good education. They don't reach a pinnacle of success from learning by osmosis. Investors understand that the market changes often and they need to keep up with the changes or else be left behind. If you are getting into real estate investing or if you already own a dozen properties, it's important to be a student of the industry.

Here are some great ways to continue learning:

- Read books written by other real estate investors.
- Stay up-to-date on industry-related news.
- Listen to podcasts about small business or real estate.
- Attend local real estate seminars and conferences.

Figure out the way you best absorb new information and start learning.

Weinhold recommends books like Rich Dad Poor Dad by Robert Kiyosaki, Loopholes of Real Estate by Garrett Sutton, and I recommend Weinhold's own Amazon best-selling 7 Money Myths That Are Killing Your Wealth Potential as good educational resources for new investors.

2) Build A Network

Rarely is success obtained when "flying solo." Even top real estate investors have someone to reach out to for advice, to review a potential deal, or to discuss what's currently going on in the market. As you build your portfolio, build your network too. Reach out to real estate investors you want to emulate. It could be as simple as asking to meet for coffee or doing a Skype call.

You'll become a better real estate investor when you are in the company of people who are better than you. In addition, the bigger your network, the more people you have to give you a head's up about potential investment opportunities.

3) Purchase Wisely

What makes someone a top real estate investor? Step one is to own properties that earn money, of course. In a best-case scenario, money is made right at the purchase of a rental property. In the beginning, getting a good deal means instant equity in the property, and starting an investment with money already made is ideal.

Top real estate investors profit off their investments because they don't overpay in the beginning, and they aren't bound to any property if the numbers don't make sense. Real estate investors know there are plenty of other investment opportunities available to go after. They also understand the benefits of leverage—when an investor uses borrowed money to increase the odds of a financial gain—and often use it to their advantage.

When these top real estate investors use leverage, also known as "other people's money," to purchase a property, they benefit in a couple of ways:

1. They increase their ability to buy a more expensive piece of real estate.
2. They can put the cash they don't spend on the deal toward additional properties.

"Maximize the use of leverage," Weinhold says. "Though I invest primarily for cash flow, long-term, buy-and-hold investors often get the greatest returns from leveraged appreciation."

4) Purchase Often

To make money investing in real estate, you need more than just one rental property. Top real estate investors have portfolios with tens or even hundreds of properties. Each property they own is just another source of monthly revenue. Besides the increased cash flow that comes with owning multiple properties, investors also achieve more flexibility and peace of mind. For example, if one rental property is vacant, it doesn't hurt the investor as much because they have other income streams from their portfolio to keep things afloat until leasing the property.

If you can't afford to buy multiple properties at once, that's OK. Start with one, build up your cash flow, and use the proceeds to buy your next property. Continue with this strategy until you own a large portfolio of properties.

Are You a Top Real Estate Investor?

A common expression used to describe real estate investing is "passive income," but most of it is not passive (unless you consider turnkey investing). Top real estate investors got to where they are because they did their homework, they kept learning, they built their network, and they kept their eyes open for their next opportunity. If you follow their habits, chances are you could wind up a top real estate investor too.

"Avoid postponing," Weinhold says. "In life, 'go and do' gets you farther than 'wait and see.'"

PROSPECTIVE PROPERTY MANAGER QUESTIONNAIRE

General Info

1. Who is the head of the office?

2. How long has the company been a property manager?

3. How many units does the company manage?

4. How many are currently vacant?

5. Who will be my property manager?

6. Will I have one specific property manager?

7. How long has my property manager been a property manager?

8. How many units does my property manager manage?

9. How many are currently vacant?

10. What is the shortest, longest and average length that tenants stay in the same property?

11. What do you offer that sets you apart from other companies?

12. How is rent paid to the owner?

13. When is rent paid to the owner?

Communication

1. What do you expect from me as the owner?

2. How often do you communicate with the owners?

3. Do you provide the owner's information to the tenant?

4. Do you have a policy about owners contacting the tenants?

5. How often do you reach out to the owners?

6. Can you give me examples of how and when you would communicate various problems?

7. What are your turnaround time on phone calls and emails from owners?

8. What are your turnaround time on phone calls and emails from tenants?

Lease Terms

1. Who are the parties on the lease?

2. Do you provide a copy of the lease to the owner, and if so, when?

3. What lengths of lease do you offer?

4. Do you do a break-out clause?

5. Do you have a rental deductible?

6. Do you do "sight unseen" leases? If yes, do you have a special addendum?

7. Who is responsible for pest control?

8. Who is responsible for lawn maintenance?

9. Who is responsible for maintaining HVAC systems?

10. Who is responsible for utilities?

11. How much move-out notice do you require?

Renewals

1. Is the lease automatically renewable?

2. What is your renewal policy?

3. Do you perform a market evaluation for every renewal?

4. How do you determine to raise the rent or keep it the same?

Advertising/Screening/Lease-Up

1. What is your advertising strategy?

2. How do you determine the recommended rental rate?

3. Do you recommend any work be done to get top dollar?

4. How long do you expect it to take to get a property rented out?

5. How quickly do you schedule showing/return calls?

6. How quickly does it take you to approve tenants and have a lease signed?

7. What is your schedule for payments when installing a tenant?

8. What is your application and screening process?

9. What are your screening requirements?

10. Do you run the tenant(s) by the owner before you approve them?

11. What do you charge for your application process?

Late Fees

1. What is your late policy?

2. What is your late fee amount?

3. Who keeps the late fees?

4. If the tenant does not pay their fees, will you still charge the owner for them?

5. How many "late" payments does it take to have a fee assessed?

Evictions

1. How many evictions did you perform last year?

2. How do you handle the eviction process?

3. Is the eviction part of the cost or is it an additional cost?

Inspections

1. Do you do a pre-inspection before the tenant move in/out?

2. How often do you do inspections during a tenant's term?

3. How do you document the inspection, and do you send it to the owners?

4. What forms do you use for the move in/out inspection?

5. Do you take video or pictures?

6. What are your criteria for what you put down on the forms?

Security Deposit/Tenant Damages

1. How do you handle the security deposit?

2. How do you charge for tenant(s) damage during their lease term?

3. If the tenant has damages that exceed the security deposit, do you come up with the documents and pursue the tenant?

4. When do you return the security deposit?

5. Do you get approval from the owner first?

6. Do you have lease language that requires the tenant to pay for any damage they cause that is not "wear and tear"?

Maintenance/Repairs

1. Do you require a maintenance deposit for each property?

2. Do you charge for a mark-up fee for maintenance?

3. Do you get multiple bids? If so, how many bids and at what threshold?

4. Is your maintenance in-house or 3rd party vendors?

5. How do you handle off-hour emergencies?

6. What do you consider emergencies?

7. Do you ask permission of the owner or fix and bill?

8. What are the largest, smallest and average annual repair costs for a single-family property over the past three years?

9. What was the reason for the largest repair cost?

10. Do you troubleshoot with your tenants when they call for repairs?

Vacancy/Turnover

1. How much time between tenants do you leave?

2. What has been your shortest, longest and average vacancy over the past 12 months?

3. What was the reason for your longest vacancy?

4. Do you show the property while the current tenant is in the property?

5. Do you have a termination clause if the property is vacant after a set period?

Fees

1. What is your monthly fee?

2. What does the monthly fee include?

3. Do you have any additional charges or fees?

4. What does my monthly charge not cover?

5. Do you charge for renewals?

6. Who keeps the fees that the tenants pay?

7. Does the owner pay any fees when the property is vacant?

Resource: americanrealpm.com

AUTHOR

John Larson is the creator of the Real Estate Cowboys and Managing Partner at American Real Estate Investments (AREI), one of the nation's largest passive income real estate investment providers. At AREI, John assists investors in building real estate portfolios in some of the best markets in the U.S. Also, AREI develops land for residential and commercial use as well as creating luxury vacation rental homes internationally.

In addition to the weekly podcast, he is a Contributing Writer at Forbes and a steady podcast guest for Think Realty, The Real Estate Guys, Joe Fairless, and Get Rich Education with Keith Weinhold.

John started in real estate at the age of 17 flipping houses with his family. He worked on the crews doing manual labor and learned what it took to renovate homes properly. From there, he became a real estate agent in Michigan and worked at the #1 brokerage in the state.

John worked with some of the largest investors in Michigan to build multi-million-dollar rental portfolios. Through the connections he made, John landed a position at a large investment fund as an Acquisitions Manager, where he focused on investment opportunities in Michigan, Missouri, and Georgia. John and his team purchased nearly 400 assets in one year.

While working in Missouri, John crossed paths with the team at American Real Estate Investments, and they were impressed by John's track record in the single-family rental space, inviting him to join their team.

John continues to help grow American Real Estate Investments into the best passive income investment provider in the country and educate through the Real Estate Cowboys brand.

areiusa.com

realestatecowboysdfw.com

www.ingramcontent.com/pod-product-compliance
Lightning Source LLC
Chambersburg PA
CBHW051332220526
45468CB00004B/1609